D0577580

SING ME A WINDOW

Elizabeth Lee O'Donnell

SING ME
A
WINDOW

Pictures by
Melissa Sweet

Morrow Junior Books/New York

To Nancy Willard, Dorothy Hole,
and Meredith Charpentier
—E. L. O'D.

To Lisa, Peter,
Noelle, and Lucas
—M. S.

Pen-and-ink, pencil, and watercolors were used for the full-color artwork.
The text type is 16-point Souvenir.

Text copyright © 1993 by Elizabeth Lee O'Donnell
Illustrations copyright © 1993 by Melissa Sweet

Printed in Hong Kong by South China Printing Company (1988) Ltd.

1   2   3   4   5   6   7   8   9   10

Library of Congress Cataloging-in-Publication Data
O'Donnell, Elizabeth Lee.
Sing me a window / Elizabeth Lee O'Donnell; illustrated by
Melissa Sweet.
p.   cm.
Summary: A child requests a bedtime song about her teddy bear and
their adventures together.
ISBN 0-688-09500-3 (trade).—ISBN 0-688-09501-1 (library)
1. Children's poetry, American. [1. Bedtime—Poetry. 2. Teddy
bears—Poetry. 3. American poetry.] I. Sweet, Melissa, ill. II. Title.
PS3565.D55S5   1993
811'.54—dc20   92-10719   CIP   AC

Sing me a song of my fat brown bear,
of that old blue ball I left on the stair.
Sing about kittens who tickle my toes.
Sing me a song so my eyes won't close.

Sing me the song my sailboat sings,
   slipping up ripples, sliding by wings.
Sing about wood ducks and dark-winged loons; and
Sing about geese making vees near the moon.

Sing me a night song,
a soft song,
a dream song.

Sing me the song the high wind sings
    when we climb to the top of the tree.
Sing how we pick the ripest red leaves
    —you and bear and me.

Sing about swinging out over the world,
   how bear is scared, but not me; and
Sing how you laugh and hug us tight
   while the wind dances leaves way out of sight.

Sing me a night song,
a soft song,
a dream song.

Sing me the secret the wind whispers low
     when we crunch through the leftover leaves.
Sing about clouds who sail with the wind,
     about stories they sing to the trees.
Sing how we taste the wind and the rain,
     how wind tastes sharp and rain tastes green.
Sing me the secret to catch the wind,
     the secret to fly to the sky.
Sing me the magic to wish me wings.
Sing me the wish; sing me the wings.

Sing me a night song,
    a soft song,
        a dream song.

Sing me the song I hear the rain sing
when thunder chases it down.
Sing how we dance in puddles and pools,
in mud, all squishy and brown.

Sing about leaves we float like boats
    on streams we wish were filled with fish; and
Sing about rainbows that climb so high
    they are lost near the edge of the sky.

Sing me a night song,
a soft song,
a dream song.

Sing me the song the storm clouds sing
    to rock the moon to sleep; and
Sing about stars who sleep beyond clouds
    and the littlest one who peeks.
Sing me the song my chocolate pot sings
    to sing me to bed and to sleep; and
Sing me a song for fat brown bear
    who's tired and nearly asleep.

Sing me a night song,
a soft song,
a dream song.

Sing me a window into the sky
   where fat brown bear and I can fly.
Sing me a window into the night
   where, after a nap in God's great lap,
     fat brown bear and I can run
      with wishing stars till night is done.

Sing shadows to stillness.

Sing thanks for the day.

Sing me the promise that dawn's on its way.